UNSOLVED MYSTERIES

the secret files

The Bermuda Triangle

Aaron Rosenberg

the rosen publishing group's
rosen central

This book is dedicated to my grandmother, Sally Rosenberg,
who never stopped believing in me. Wherever you are, Grandma,
I hope you're as proud of me as I am of you.

Published in 2002 by The Rosen Publishing Group, Inc.
29 East 21st Street, New York, NY 10010

First Edition

Library of Congress Cataloging-in-Publication Data

Rosenberg, Aaron.
The Bermuda Triangle / by Aaron Rosenberg.— 1st ed.
p. cm. — (Unsolved mysteries)
Includes bibliographical references (p.).
Summary: Traces the history of the Bermuda Triangle, surveying some of the disappearances in that area and some of the many theories surrounding it.
ISBN 0-8239-3560-4 (lib. bdg.)
1. Bermuda Triangle—Juvenile literature. [1. Bermuda Triangle.] I. Title.
II. Unsolved mysteries (Rosen Publishing Group)
G558 .R67 2001
001.94—dc21

2001003788

Manufactured in the United States of America

Contents

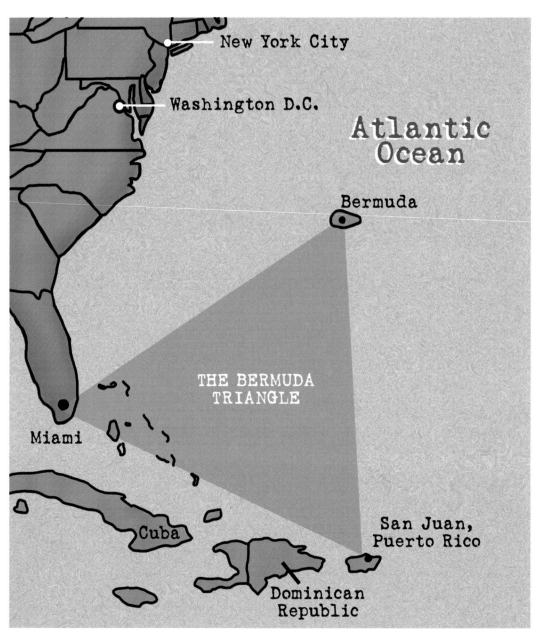

The Bermuda Triangle lies off the southeast coast of the United States.

1

Just the Facts

The Twilight Zone. The Hoodoo Sea. The Limbo of the Lost. The Devil's Triangle. The Magic Rhombus. The Port of Missing Ships. The Triangle of Death. These are all names given to the same mysterious location, a triangular area of ocean that today is called the Bermuda Triangle. The Bermuda Triangle has a long and perilous history, and can still send a shiver through sailors and aviators.

Oddly enough, the United States Board of Geographic Names does not recognize the Bermuda Triangle as an official name, and it does not have an official file on the area. And, because it is part of a larger body of water, the Triangle does not have any specific boundaries or markers.

Usually the Triangle is described as the triangular area between the points of Miami, Florida, the island of Bermuda, and San Juan,

Puerto Rico—roughly 500,000 square miles of the Atlantic Ocean. Some say that it stretches as far north as the coast of Virginia and south to the shore of Cuba or the Dominican Republic. Some estimates for the Triangle range as high as 1.5 million square miles in area.

Two facts are certain. The Bermuda Triangle lies in the Atlantic Ocean, off the southeastern coast of the United States. It has been the site of an unusually high number of bizarre disappearances. Boats, planes, and people have all vanished there without a trace.

To make matters more complicated, the Bermuda Triangle encompasses some of the most popular tourist locations in the world. It has always seen a great deal of water traffic (and later, in the twentieth century, air traffic as well), starting with the earliest recorded account in 1492 when Christopher Columbus sailed through it to get to the New World. The Triangle's southeastern point is also not that far from the birthplace of most of the Atlantic Ocean hurricanes, which form off the northwest coast of Africa, and is often home to its own type of spectacular and unpredictable storms. In fact, a single storm in the region of the Triangle can produce as much as ten inches of rain in just a matter of hours. The Gulf Stream runs through the Triangle, altering the water currents in that area, and beneath the

The Bermuda islands mark the northernmost point of "the Devil's Triangle."

Triangle's surface lie some of the Atlantic's deepest waters—as deep as 30,000 feet! Just to add to the watery confusion, scientists recently discovered an ocean current running hundreds of feet beneath the Gulf Stream but going in the opposite direction!

There's yet another oddity to the Bermuda Triangle. In the rest of the world, there are two measurements of "north." The first is called magnetic north. This is the direction seen on a compass. The second is called true north. This is the actual geographic direction. Normally, the two measurements of north are off by as much as 20 degrees. This is known as compass variation, and compasses have to be adjusted to account for the difference. But the Bermuda Triangle is one of only two spots on the planet where magnetic north and true north are perfectly aligned.

There's another strange area not too far from the Bermuda Triangle. This is called the Sargasso Sea after its floating, tangled jungles of sargassum seaweed. The Sargasso Sea lies east of Bermuda and south of the Gulf Stream, in the middle of the Atlantic. It does overlap the Bermuda Triangle at its northwestern edge and the Triangle's easternmost side, but the Sargasso is over two million square miles of ocean, four times the generally accepted size of the Triangle. Despite this, the Bermuda Triangle is often linked to the Sargasso Sea, and at times the two are even considered one and the same. Part of this confusion is probably due to the Sargasso's own oddity—in addition to its seaweed jungle, its waters are warm and constantly swirl clockwise, despite a lack of wind.

Actually, very few facts are known about the Bermuda Triangle. This only serves to increase everyone's interest, of course. Unsolved mysteries always attract attention, particularly when there may be undisclosed secrets as well.

2
Early Stories

Early sea explorers wrote in their journals of strange occurrences and bizarre events that seemed to make no sense. Many of these events took place in or near the Sargasso Sea and the Bermuda Triangle.

The first recorded incident in the Bermuda Triangle was written by one of the most famous sailors of all time: Christopher Columbus. In 1492, Columbus was on his famous journey, which would eventually lead him to the West Indies. He noted that the ship's compass was acting strangely and giving inaccurate readings, and at one point he saw a great ball of fire shoot across the sky and crash into the sea. Columbus was under a great deal of pressure at the time. His crew had begun to panic because there was no land in sight and the ship had only a limited amount of food and water, some of which had to be saved for the journey home. The last thing that Columbus would have wanted to do was to point out weird readings or fireballs to his crew.

But there were other witnesses. On October 11, Columbus and one of his crewmen both saw a light over the water, one that vanished quickly. Only hours later, the expedition spotted land: the islands of the West Indies. While none of his three ships disappeared or crashed, the records of his bizarre sightings did add to notions that the waters in that area were not exactly ordinary, and possibly even dangerous.

And then the recorded disappearances began.

In 1609, a sailing ship called the *Sea Venture* disappeared right off the coast of Bermuda. A rescue boat was sent after it,

but that one vanished as well. These are the earliest known disappearances in the Bermuda Triangle, but they were only the beginning.

A little over a hundred years went by

Christopher Columbus was the first sailor to record unusual events while sailing through the Bermuda Triangle.

without any major problems. But then, in 1750, three Spanish galleons accompanying the *Nuestra Señora de Guadalupe* disappeared off the coast of North Carolina.

It wasn't until the nineteenth century that the disappearances began happening in earnest. In 1812, sixty-two years after the Spanish galleons vanished, the *Patriot,* an American packet ship, disappeared in the Gulf Stream. This caused a great deal of excitement because the missing ship was carrying Vice President Aaron Burr's daughter. Two years later, in 1814, the U.S. warship *Wasp* vanished off the coast of South Carolina.

The next incident to capture people's attention and imagination was not a disappearance but a weird reappearance. In 1840, the French vessel the *Rosalie* was found drifting in the Triangle. Her sails were set and she was undamaged, but she was utterly unmanned. Her cargo was untouched. Clearly she hadn't been set upon by pirates. With no sign of damage, it makes no sense to think that some emergency forced an evacuation. No trace of her passengers or crew was ever found.

The *Rosalie* was not the most famous unmanned ship, however. That honor goes to another of the great names in sailing

Several nineteenth-century ships disappeared in the Bermuda Triangle's waters.

history: the *Mary Celeste.* On November 7, 1872, the *Mary Celeste* left New York Harbor and headed for Genoa, Italy. It was carrying a cargo of industrial alcohol, the type used for medicinal and other purposes unrelated to drinking. Captain Benjamin Spooner Briggs was in control of the vessel. Also on board were his wife, Sarah, his two-year-old daughter, and eight crewmen. On December 4, 1872, the *Dei Gratia* found the *Mary Celeste* floating in the Atlantic Ocean. One lifeboat was missing, as were the people, but otherwise the ship was intact and everything was properly stowed, including personal belongings. Whatever had driven the captain, his family, and his crew to leave had apparently forced them to move quickly. The last position recorded in the *Mary Celeste*'s log put her roughly 100 miles west of the Azores, islands off the coast of Portugal, which meant she would have passed near or through the Bermuda Triangle, almost 400 miles off course. However, there are some who claim that the *Mary Celeste* was never in the Triangle and that her fate had nothing mysterious about it. They claim that the Triangle element was added later, after it had caught everyone's attention.

And the fact remains that the mystery of the fate of the captain and crew of the *Mary Celeste* has never been solved.

3

The Birth of a Name

Where does the name "Bermuda Triangle" come from? Surprisingly, even though that area of the Atlantic has featured heavily in folktales and legends—as well as in the horror stories of sailors—the Bermuda Triangle's name isn't even a century old. In fact, it wasn't until the twentieth century that the public began to hear of it. In 1950, a reporter named E. V. W. Jones mentioned the area in an Associated Press dispatch. He talked about the mysterious disappearances of ships and planes between Bermuda and the Florida coast. That got the public's attention!

Two years later, another reporter, George X. Sand, wrote an article for *Fate* magazine, talking about a "series of strange marine disappearances, each leaving no trace whatever, that have taken place in the past few years" in a "watery triangle bounded roughly by Florida, Bermuda and Puerto Rico."

Now the public was really interested. Soon others began writing about the area as well. M. K. Jessup, in his book *The Case for the UFO,* claimed that the disappearances were actually alien abductions. Donald E. Kyhoe said much the same in his 1955 book, *The Flying Saucer Conspiracy.* The Triangle began to appear in science fiction stories, particularly with this idea of alien involvement.

Then, in February of 1964, a writer named Vincent Gaddis wrote a piece for the magazine *Argosy,* in which he discussed "the Deadly Bermuda Triangle" and what a large number of disappearances the area had seen—or perhaps had caused. Gaddis later expanded the article into a book, called *Invisible Horizons: True Mysteries of the Sea.* People who worked for *Argosy* were delighted with the article and the readers' enthusiastic response, and ran more details and follow-ups. A letter in their May 1964 issue talked about a plane that had flown over the area in 1944 and never returned. In August of 1968, *Argosy*'s cover story was "The Spreading Mystery of the Bermuda Triangle."

The Triangle now not only had its name, but had caught public interest, and it continued to do so. In 1969, John Wallace Spencer wrote a book called *Limbo of the Lost,* which was

Skeptics claim that most lost vessels are the result of storms.

specifically about the Triangle. But what really established the Bermuda Triangle as a phenomenon was the feature documentary *The Devil's Triangle,* which was released in 1971, and a book called *The Bermuda Triangle,* which was written by Charles Berlitz and published in 1974. Berlitz has been accused of manipulating his readers, never offering any concrete answers, and deliberately exaggerating and even fabricating details. But no matter what critics said, *The Bermuda Triangle* quickly became a best-seller, and soon almost everyone was talking about the Bermuda Triangle and its dangerous, or maybe even supernatural, nature.

4

The Twentieth-
Century Curse

The Bermuda Triangle did not become any less dangerous in the twentieth century—far from it. As more and more ships crossed the Atlantic every year, more and more ships disappeared into the Triangle, never to be seen again. The Triangle doesn't seem to care about nationality, either; ships from all over the world have been its victims.

In 1902, the German vessel *Freya* was found in the region of the Triangle. It was listing badly to one side, part of its mast was gone, and its crew had vanished.

In March 1918, the USS *Cyclops,* captained by Lieutenant Commander George W. Worley, left Barbados for Baltimore. Days later, with the ship long overdue, a massive search was launched. But no trace of the *Cyclops* was ever found. It was the largest ship in the navy, and it had left Barbados with 300 people on board.

The USS *Cyclops* was the largest ship in the navy when it vanished in 1918.

In 1924, the Japanese freighter *Raifucu Maru* radioed for help, but the ship and its crew were never found. In 1941, the USS *Cyclops*'s two sister ships, *Proteus* and *Nereus*, both vanished while traveling from the Virgin Islands to the United States—one month apart. In 1944, it was a Cuban freighter, the *Rubicon,* that encountered the mystery of the Triangle. The ship was found, but the only member of its crew remaining on board was a dog.

As airplane travel became more common toward the mid-twentieth century, and both passenger and cargo flights began to cross the Atlantic, the Triangle began claiming airplanes as well as ships.

Lieutenant Commander George W. Worley captained the ill-fated *Cyclops*.

In 1945, the most famous of all the Bermuda Triangle disappearances took place. This was the mystery of Flight 19. It began without any unusual incidents. On December 5, 1945, Flight 19 left the Fort Lauderdale navy air base on a routine training mission. Lieutenant Charles Taylor, an experienced pilot and instructor, was patrol leader. He was flying a navy Avenger bomber. Four other Avengers flew with him, each one under the control of a rookie pilot. The training mission itself, a test bombing run followed by several turns, was a complete success.

But on the return flight, Taylor began to have some strange difficulties. He radioed the base and informed them that his compass was no longer working properly and that he was confused as to the flight's current location and direction. He attempted to navigate by using landmarks, but night was falling and visibility dropped rapidly.

Then a storm set in, and the weather worsened. Fort Lauderdale was still in contact with Taylor, but the storm made communication difficult. Taylor informed the base that he was over the Gulf of Mexico and turned Flight 19 east to search for land. Unfortunately, he was probably mistaken and in fact turned away from land and back out over the Atlantic. The Avengers had only six hours worth of fuel, and as the night deepened, the navy grew more concerned. Finally, they dispatched several planes to search for the missing flight, including a Martin Mariner. The Mariner had an enormous gas tank and could fly for twelve hours without refueling. It was the perfect plane for a long search. But the Mariner never returned. Neither did Flight 19.

Critics claim that it wasn't so unusual for planes to have difficulties. They point out that four of the five Avengers were piloted by rookies. They also claim that Taylor was already confused that day, and he simply got disoriented. But no one can explain what happened to the planes and the pilots. Each Avenger had a three-man life raft and a two-man crew, but no life rafts were ever found. Nor were there any other traces of the Avengers or their crews. The Triangle had apparently simply swallowed them up. The mystery of Flight 19, more than any other event, drew attention to the Bermuda Triangle.

U.S. Air Force Avengers were used
for training missions over the
Bermuda Triangle.

The story ran in all the papers, and soon everyone was talking about the Triangle and its appetite for ships and planes.

The mystery of the Bermuda Triangle increased in 1948. The airplane *Star Tiger* disappeared en route to Bermuda, only moments after radioing ground crew that they would arrive on schedule. A year later, the *Star Tiger*'s sister plane, the *Star Ariel,* also disappeared while traveling from Bermuda to Jamaica. Needless to say, this new pair of disappearances added to the Bermuda Triangle's fame—or maybe that should be infamy.

5
Logical Explanations

As happens with any bizarre situation, people want to find a comforting answer to the mystery. They have offered many different theories about the Bermuda Triangle and the various disappearances. Many of the theories come from scientists and are based on facts. Other theories are more imaginative.

HUMAN ERROR

The most commonly mentioned theory is simply that the disappearances were caused by simple human error. After all, the Bermuda Triangle includes such popular places as Miami and Bermuda. Many of the people who travel through the area are on vacation. They may be partying and possibly drunk or simply not really paying attention to what they're doing. They sometimes take trips in boats that were never meant to handle ocean currents, or go sailing late at night without proper lighting or maps, and without any experience in or knowledge of the area. Such careless pleasure seekers often find something far more dangerous than a little late-night fun: They find death on the high seas.

EXAGGERATION

Some skeptical people say the answer to the Bermuda Triangle's string of bizarre disappearances is that they weren't as bizarre as they seem. These skeptics claim that the mystery is nothing but exaggeration and fabrication, whether deliberate or simply enthusiastic.

In 1975, an Arizona librarian named Larry Kusche decided to investigate the claims about the Bermuda Triangle. He published his findings in a book called *The Bermuda Triangle Mystery Solved.* In it, Kusche claimed that many of the strange accidents in the Triangle were exaggerated. He stated that ships that had vanished in calm waters actually went down in raging storms, that boats that had vanished without a trace had in fact been recovered, and that ships that had supposedly disappeared in the Triangle had, in fact, never been anywhere near it.

Skeptics claim that freak storms are among the likely causes of lost ships within the Bermuda Triangle.

In the same year, the editor of *Fate* magazine looked over accident reports from oceans around the world from the famous British insurance company Lloyd's of London. What the editor found was that the Bermuda Triangle's accident rate was no higher than anywhere else. The United States Coast Guard confirms this, saying that it has never been impressed by claims of the Triangle's danger or its supernatural nature.

COMPASS VARIATION

The Bermuda Triangle is a dangerous place for navigators, even without any supernatural menace. Part of that is its odd lack of compass variation. Normally a navigator has to consider the difference between the compass's north and true north, or else he or she could wind up guiding a boat or plane off course. In the Bermuda Triangle, where magnetic north and true north actually match, navigators have to remember not to compensate. If they automatically compensate for a variation that does not exist, they will wind up off course. In the middle of the ocean, such a miscalculation can be fatal.

THE GULF STREAM

Another major factor to be considered in the mystery of the Bermuda Triangle is the Gulf Stream. This current flows steadily northeast, from the tip of Florida up the eastern seaboard and then across the Atlantic to the United Kingdom. It divides the cold Atlantic waters from the warm Sargasso Sea, and it accounts for the fog in London, as well as the more moderate temperatures in most of Europe. Thanks to the warmth of the Gulf Stream, parts of Europe that are on the same latitude as New England and Canada can grow even tropical plants like palm trees.

The Gulf Stream is not only warm and steady, it is very fast and very turbulent. An inexperienced pilot could easily lose control and be carried off course, winding up north and east of the right destination. The speed of the Gulf Stream could also quickly wash away any debris, explaining why ships and planes have vanished without a trace; debris caught in the Gulf Stream has wound up farther away in the North Atlantic.

WEATHER CONDITIONS

Weather, some people say, could also be a major factor in the mystery of the Bermuda Triangle. In the Triangle, severe storms can form without warning and dissipate completely before ever reaching shore. These storms are often too small and swiftly forming for meteorologists to predict accurately. Known as meso-meteorological storms, they can include tornadoes, thunderstorms, and tropical cyclones.

In severe weather, visibility can drop drastically, so fast that planes can literally dive into the ocean without the pilots realizing what's happening. Giant waves can be stirred up by the storms, large enough to engulf a ship and drag it under. The electricity generated by thunderstorms can short out communications and guidance systems, leaving ships and planes powerless and blind. A ship or plane might disappear in such a storm, and then, moments later, the storm might pass, leaving nothing but calm waters behind.

WATER ABOVE BUT EARTH BELOW

One interesting theory is that the Bermuda Triangle is subject to earth-quakes. Even though they would take place on the ocean floor, miles below the surface, the resulting vibrations could affect water currents up above, generating sudden waves and even whirlpools. Without sophisticated equipment to detect seismic activity—and equipment specially designed to penetrate to the ocean floor—ships could easily be swamped by the sudden shifts in pressure and wave activity.

Even without earthquakes, whirlpools can be deadly to ships. Whirlpools are created by conflicting currents in the water, and they can appear out of nowhere. A strong whirlpool can pull in a medium-sized ship and suck it under the water in just a few hours. Lifeboats would also be pulled under, of course, limiting the possibility of survivors or witnesses.

SPATIAL DISORIENTATION

Many of the Bermuda Triangle stories include references to pilots who can't see anything, report clear weather conditions, or simply say that things look strange. This may in fact be the result of spatial disorientation, a very real danger often mentioned by the Federal Aviation Administration (FAA).

Our sense of balance comes from the position of fluid and tiny hairs in our inner ears. Apparently, this inner ear fluid is affected by quick changes, but not by a steady and continual change. If you tilt your head sharply to one side, you will notice a shift in your sense of balance. But if you slowly tilt your head to one side and hold it that way, the shift will be less sudden, and eventually you will not have any difficulty holding your head to the side while keeping your balance.

This is what can happen to pilots. If a plane goes into a sudden dive, the pilot would know he was diving. However, if he continued to dive, after a minute his inner ear would compensate, and he would feel, wrongly, as if he'd leveled off again.

Normally, this is not a problem for pilots: They have instruments to tell them altitude and angle, and during a clear day, they can always use visual cues as well. But at night, over the ocean, there is little to see and almost no visual cues. The dark sky often blends into the dark water, so much so that you cannot tell where your horizon is. If you have lost your instruments or are flying without instruments, or if you don't believe what your instruments are telling you, this can mean that you're flying right into the ocean without even realizing it. And the Bermuda Triangle not only doesn't offer many visual cues, its frequent storms can completely block visibility, forcing a pilot to rely on any working instruments and on gut feeling. And, as previously discussed, gut feeling isn't reliable when the inner ear is confused.

Alcohol also throws off the sense of balance, as well as the sense of judgment. As can be the case with those who have gone partying on boats when they've had too much to drink, any pilot flying over the ocean under the influence of alcohol stands a good chance of wandering into the Triangle and never returning.

BUBBLES FROM BELOW

One of the more unusual scientific theories concerning the Bermuda Triangle has to do with bubbles of gas. The theory states that pockets of methane gas are released from the ocean floor. Methane causes the water in that area to become less dense. This means that buoyancy there drops suddenly. If a boat was directly over a large amount of methane, the boat would lose its buoyancy and sink quickly.

This is not as bizarre as it might sound. Scientists say the Bermuda Triangle is high in natural methane hydrates. This means that released bubbles of methane gas could occur at any time, and any ship caught by enough of them could, indeed, find itself quickly sinking to the ocean floor.

6

Beyond the Rational

Can the mystery of the Bermuda Triangle be so easily explained away by sudden storms or mere coincidence? Some people don't think that's possible. After all, scientists have been arguing over the area for decades, yet no one theory has ever been proven, let alone generally accepted.

This is not so surprising. After all, not everything in life can be proven or explained. But people continue to try. The Bermuda Triangle has for centuries been a magnet for the imagination, and people other than scientists have suggested a wide variety of reasons for the area's effect on boats and planes. Some of these use bits of science or logic, but many rely upon bizarre situations that we cannot prove or disprove. Could they be right? Anything is possible.

ABDUCTION

Did aliens abduct those missing ships and planes? Stories of alien sightings, and of abductions of unfortunate humans, have been recorded for centuries, as have Triangle disappearances. Abductions seem to take place in isolated areas, such as the middle of the Atlantic Ocean. Many UFO sightings and abductions involve bizarre power failures; several of the vanished planes and boats, including Flight 19, reported equipment failure. Could aliens have targeted the Triangle as a likely collection area and made off with ships and boats—and their passengers—over the centuries? It would explain how they vanished without a trace.

Or perhaps UFOs are the cause, but not a deliberate one. After all, not every alien encounter ends in abduction and experimentation. What if a UFO had crashed into the Bermuda Triangle at some point? After all, scientists say the area is dangerous to flying ships. A UFO,

presumably with advanced technology, would probably run on some alternate power source we haven't figured out yet. It could still work even after such a crash, even if the crew themselves were killed. If the alien vessel were set up to automatically

Some people have offered UFO abduction theories to explain Bermuda Triangle disappearances.

block signals within range in order to avoid detection, that technology might still be operational. This would mean ships passing nearby and planes flying overhead would suddenly lose power and/or navigation, and would crash before they could find a way around the problem.

Or what if the aliens have landed? They would need a base of operations, and why assume they've set one up on land? If their ship can handle outer space, surely it can also function under water. Perhaps their base is in the Atlantic Ocean, between Miami, Bermuda, and Puerto Rico, which would place it at the heart of the Triangle. Most people put up a fence around their home for privacy. Perhaps the aliens have done the same thing, using not a physical fence but some sort of energy field that knocks out any electronics in the immediate area, to prevent people from scanning for and locating them.

THE PHILADELPHIA EXPERIMENT

What if humanity is to blame for the Bermuda Triangle? Often we meddle with things we don't really understand; scientists, many people believe, are particularly guilty of this fault. Such experimenting can lead to tremendous breakthroughs, but it can also lead to disasters.

In 1943, the Philadelphia Naval Yard was supposedly home to a secret experiment. American scientists were testing the effects of a strong magnetic field on a ship, the USS *Eldridge,* using powerful generators to create an intense field around the vessel. Their goal was apparently to render the ship invisible, but the results were very different. The ship, and all its crew, supposedly disappeared. They were later reported in Norfolk, Virginia, but they vanished there as well. What if the Philadelphia Experiment succeeded, but not in creating invisibility? What if, instead, it created some sort of gateway through time and space? Any ships or planes that accidentally passed through that portal would find themselves transported into the past or the future. That would explain why we've never found remains of them. Either the wrecks have fallen apart from thousands of years of erosion, or we haven't caught up to them yet. And since the portal runs through time as well as space, it could have caused all those disappearances over the centuries. The gateway might exist throughout time, and those ships were also pulled either into the past or somewhere into our future!

Even if the experiment was a failure, it might still explain the Triangle. Powerful magnets were involved. What if they created an

The Philadelphia Naval Yard was reportedly home to an electromagnetic experiment that some claimed caused the disappearance of a navy ship.

area of magnetic instability, where magnetism goes haywire? Every electronic device flying or sailing through it could be affected. And if the area is unstable, it might fluctuate, which would explain why some ships and planes aren't affected (they passed by when the field was weaker, so it didn't interfere with them). The Bermuda Triangle does have an unusual magnetic field; it might be stranger than scientists admit. Of course, the navy denies the Philadelphia Experiment altogether, but they could simply be covering up the truth.

LOST CITY

Perhaps the answer lies not in modern failures but in an ancient success. The lost city of Atlantis is supposedly sunken thousands of feet below the water's surface, but no one is sure exactly where. What if its final resting place lies within the Bermuda Triangle? Stories of Atlantis say that it was extremely advanced for its time and had technologies we still have not mastered. Many of the people who have studied the Atlantis tales think that the Atlanteans used some sort of crystals, somehow harnessing their energies. Some crystals are extremely tough and can resist a tremendous amount of damage; they could have survived the city's destruction and still be intact at the bottom of the ocean. But what if centuries of immersion in seawater have altered the structure of the crystals, so that they now broadcast energies that interfere with the instruments and engines of passing boats and planes? If this is true, two of mankind's most powerful mysteries are actually one and the same, and the Bermuda Triangle is a signpost leading to Atlantis itself. Weird columns do lie in the water off Bermuda, and though scientists claim that these are perfectly natural geological structures, there are those who state that they are part of the lost city.

Some speculate that the Triangle is the grave of Atlantis, the famous lost city.

TWISTER

What if bizarre weather was to blame for the disappearances in the Bermuda Triangle? A psychic named Ed Snedeker claimed that the Bermuda Triangle was caused by twisters. According to him, these twisting tunnels, like tornado funnels, exist all around us, but they're invisible to the naked eye. These funnels move from north to south through the Bermuda Triangle, sucking up aircraft, ships, and people, and carrying them off, depositing them finally at some hidden location in the Atlantic. Weather patterns are unpredictable, and the Triangle is well known to be the site of fabulous storms appearing out of nowhere. Could these funnels exist, and were those missing ships and planes unlucky enough to be in their paths? If so, somewhere there is a resting place for all those vessels. If we can ever predict the movement of those funnels, we might be able to find the wreckage all at once.

NATURE'S STARGATES

Dr. Michael Preisinger, a German historian and scuba diver, has proposed another possibility, one that might actually explain Snedeker's claims. Preisinger believes the Bermuda Triangle is the site of naturally occurring wormholes, miniature black holes that essentially tunnel through space. These wormholes appear and disappear at random, but they cause magnetic anomalies and their gravitational pull (similar to that of a full-sized black hole) would be strong enough to absorb any ships or planes in the vicinity. They would be crushed to microscopic size as they passed through the hole's event horizon. Water and air would also be pulled in, and scientists have recently learned that some black holes spin. If the wormholes did the same, they could create funnels, eerily close to Snedeker's invisible tunnels. Have scientists and psychics hit upon the right answer from opposite directions?

DAMNATION ALLEY

Perhaps the Bermuda Triangle is truly otherworldly, but in a super-natural sense rather than an extraterrestrial one. After all, it is also known as the Devil's Triangle. What if, as some people believe, biblical stories are literally true? In that case, Good and Evil are real, as are Heaven and Hell, and you need to do good deeds to go to Heaven.

But if you want to reach Hell, you may only need to sail or fly over the Atlantic between Florida and Bermuda. Those who have been lost in the Bermuda Triangle may have passed through the Gates of Hell and are now damned for all eternity—poor lost souls who were simply in the wrong place at the wrong time.

Or perhaps the Triangle is more than a gateway; perhaps it is Hell itself, and those lost souls are still trapped in there somewhere where we cannot see them, caught in eternal agony. Not everyone who passes through the Devil's Triangle disappears, of course, but perhaps those who did had committed sins and thus were damned. Perhaps this is a way to make mankind doubt and fear. Both techniques would work to the Devil's advantage.

PRIVACY SCREEN

Perhaps some of the previous theories are partially right: the Triangle is a privacy screen, like a fence. But it's made by humanity, not by aliens. Various world governments have secret projects, things they don't want anyone else to see. What if one or more of these governments built a device to generate an electrical field around the Triangle in order to hide their activities? Even if the field doesn't stop every ship, it makes travelers wary and less likely to intrude. Perhaps we've never been able to pinpoint it because we can't establish exactly where each ship or plane disappeared.

This would explain why the United States Navy denies the existence of the Bermuda Triangle and claims that nothing strange has ever occurred there: They're in on the deception and covering up the truth.

THE MYSTERY REMAINS

Are any of the previously discussed theories correct? Can there be some sort of cover-up about the truth, or does everyone lack the answers? At this point, it does seem to be anyone's guess as to why the Bermuda Triangle exists and to what really happened to all those boats and planes. New theories are created every day, and perhaps some day one of them will be proven correct.

In the meantime, the Bermuda Triangle remains one of the biggest unsolved mysteries. Is it a deliberate mystery? If there really is some sort of government cover-up, then the Bermuda Triangle truly is one of the world's strangest secret files.

Glossary

Atlantis The fabled lost city, supposedly a place of peace and knowledge, that sank without a trace into the ocean.

Bermuda Triangle The name commonly used for the triangular area of the Atlantic Ocean between Miami, Florida, Bermuda, and San Juan, Puerto Rico. This area is famous for the disappearance of ships and planes.

black hole An area of space that has collapsed in on itself, creating a funnel effect; everything in the vicinity is pulled in by the black hole's powerful gravitational field and crushed as it passes through the event horizon.

compass variation A technique used by navigators to compensate for the difference between magnetic north (on a compass) and true (geographic) north.

Devil's Triangle Another name for the Bermuda Triangle, popularized by a 1971 documentary.

Flight 19 The most famous Bermuda Triangle incident; a navy flight of five bomber planes, all of which vanished without a trace on December 5, 1945.

Gulf Stream A powerful current that runs northeast across the Atlantic Ocean.

Mary Celeste A sailing ship that was found one month after it set sail, with no one left on board; possibly the most famous sea disappearance of all time.

Philadelphia Experiment A top-secret navy experiment that supposedly took place in 1943 in the Philadelphia Naval Yards. This experiment is said to have used magnetic fields in an attempt to render ships invisible to radar and sight.

Sargasso Sea An unusual area of the Atlantic Ocean that overlaps the Bermuda Triangle slightly. The waters in the Sargasso Sea are warmer than in surrounding areas and swirl clockwise even in calm weather.

wormhole A miniature black hole, or a theorized tunnel through space and time.

For More Information

WEB SITES

Due to the changing nature of Internet links, the Rosen Publishing Group, Inc., has developed an online list of Web sites related to the subject of this book. This site is updated regularly. Please use this link to access the list:

http://www.rosenlinks.com/um/betr

The Bermuda Triangle.Org
http://www.bermuda-triangle.org

Bermuda Triangle Page
http://blindkat.tripod.com/triangle/tri.html

The Loss of Flight 19
Prepared by the U.S. Naval Historical Center
http://www.history.navy.mil/faqs/faq15-1.htm

True North/Magnetic North?
http://www.bermuda-triangle.org/Theories/True_North_
    Magnetic_North_/true_north_magnetic_north_.html

VIDEOS

The Bermuda Triangle. Video release of a 1975 film by WGBH
    Educational Foundation and BBC Enterprises Ltd.
The Bermuda Triangle. The Learning Channel, 2001.
The Case of the Bermuda Triangle. BBC-TV, Vestron Video, 1988.
The Devil's Triangle. The History Channel, 2001.

For Further Reading

Berlitz, Charles. *The Bermuda Triangle.* Garden City, NY: Doubleday, 1974.

Gaddis, Vincent H. *Invisible Horizons: True Mysteries of the Sea.* Philadelphia: Chilton Books, 1965.

Gilbreath, Alice. *River in the Ocean: The Story of the Gulf Stream.* Minneapolis, MN: Dillon Press, 1986

Kusche, Larry. *The Bermuda Triangle Mystery Solved.* Buffalo, NY: Prometheus Books, 1995.

Kusche, Larry. *The Disappearance of Flight 19.* New York: Harper & Row, 1980.

Rosenberg, Howard L. "Exorcizing the Devil's Triangle." *Sealift,* No. 6, June 1974, pp. 11–15.

Whipple, A. B. C. *Restless Oceans.* Alexandria, VA: Time-Life Books, 1983.

Index

ABOUT THE AUTHOR

Aaron Rosenberg was born in New Jersey, grew up in New Orleans, and now lives in New York. He has taught college English, worked in corporate graphics, and now runs his own game publishing company. He has written short stories, poems, essays, articles, novels, and role-playing games.

PHOTO CREDITS

SERIES DESIGN AND LAYOUT

Geri Giordano